Charles Darwin

찰스 다윈

Biography Comic
who? ⑫ Charles Darwin

초판 1쇄 인쇄 2011년 4월 8일
초판 1쇄 발행 2011년 4월 15일

글 안형모
그림 스튜디오 청비
번역 채드 워커
감수 김수희
펴낸이 김선식

Chief Story Creator 김정미
Story Creator 채정은
Design Creator 김경민
Marketing Creator 신문수

Brand Creative Story Team 김정미, 채정은, 박혜연
Creative Design Dept. 최부돈, 황정민, 김태수, 조혜상, 이성희, 김경민
Creative Marketing Dept. 모계영, 이주화, 김하늘, 신문수
Communication Team 서선행, 김선준, 박혜원, 전아름
Contents Rights Team 이정순, 김미영
New Business Team 우재오
Creative Management Team 김성자, 김미현, 김유미, 정연주, 서여주, 권송이
Outsourcing 김혜령

펴낸곳 (주)다산북스
주소 서울시 마포구 서교동 395-27번지
전화 02-702-1724(기획편집) 02-703-1725(마케팅) 02-704-1724(경영지원)
팩스 02-703-2219
이메일 dasanbooks@hanmail.net
홈페이지 www.dasanbooks.com
출판등록 2005년 12월 23일 제313-2005-00277호

필름 출력 스크린그래픽센타 **종이** 월드페이퍼(주) **인쇄·제본** (주)현문

ISBN 978-89-6370-515-6 14740
SET 978-89-6370-438-8

who?
Charles Darwin
찰스 다윈

글 **안형모** | 그림 **스튜디오 청비** | 번역 **채드 워커** | 감수 **김수희**

Dasan Kid

Charles Darwin

British scientist, February 12, 1809~ April 19, 1882

Charles Darwin was born in Shrewsbury, England. Although he entered Edinburgh University to study medicine, he discovered he wasn't suited to be a doctor and dropped out after only two years. At his father's urging, he entered Cambridge University and majored in theology.

But Darwin, who, from the time he was small, only had an interest in plants and animals. He was more eager to spend his time at Cambridge collecting insects and exploring nature than studying theology. The botanist Professor Henslow took notice of Darwin and recommended him as a naturalist to travel on the English Royal Navy survey ship, the *Beagle.*

Darwin thoroughly explored South America and numerous South Pacific islands and he discovered a clue to his theory of evolution on the Galapagos Islands. The Galapagos Islands consists of 16 islands and a number of reefs. Darwin discovered that each island had a different environment and that the same species of animals that lived on different islands were of slightly different varieties.

After returning from the voyage in 1839, Darwin organized all the observational records he collected throughout his journey and published them as *The Voyage of the Beagle.* Darwin grew ill and moved into the Down House located in the outskirts of London, in Kent. There, Darwin organized materials related to his theory of evolution and began to write.

Then, in 1859, *The Origin of Species* was finally published. By 1860, the book had sparked controversy related to the theory of evolution. Scholars like Huxley and Hooker fervently supported Darwin's position and disputed their views with their opponents.

This resulted in *The Origin of Species* being published all around the world, with Darwin's view gaining recognition. Darwin continued researching and writing into his 70s, but finally succumbed to illness in 1882, when he passed away at his home. Darwin's theory of evolution was revolutionary, influencing the formation of mankind's worldview.

찰스 다윈

영국의 생물학자, 1809년 2월 12일~1882년 4월 19일

찰스 다윈은 1809년 영국 슈루즈버리에서 태어났습니다. 에든버러 대학에 입학해 의학을 배우지만 적성에 맞지 않아 2년 만에 중퇴를 하고, 아버지의 권유로 케임브리지 대학에 입학하여 신학을 공부합니다.

어릴 적부터 동식물에 관심이 많았던 다윈은 이곳에서 신학 공부보다는 곤충 수집과 자연을 탐구하는 일에 더 매진하였습니다. 그런 다윈을 눈여겨보던 식물학 교수 헨슬로는 다윈을 영국 해군 측량선인 비글호의 박물학자로 추천합니다.

남아메리카와 남태평양의 여러 섬을 두루 탐사한 다윈은 갈라파고스 제도를 탐사하던 중 진화론의 실마리를 찾게 됩니다. 갈라파고스 제도는 16개의 섬과 몇 개의 암초들로 이루어져 있었는데, 각각 다른 환경의 처해 있는 섬들과 거기에서 살아가는 같은 계통의 생물에서 사소한 변이의 차이가 있는 것을 발견한 것입니다.

1839년 항해에서 돌아온 다윈은 여행을 하는 동안 자신이 써 왔던 관찰 기록들을 정리해 〈비글호 항해기〉를 출간하였습니다. 그러나 그후 급격히 건강이 나빠져, 런던 인근의 시골에 살면서 진화론에 대한 논문을 쓰기 시작합니다.

그리고 1859년, 마침내 〈종의 기원〉을 출간합니다. 이 책의 출판을 계기로 1860년 옥스퍼드 대학에서 진화론에 관한 논쟁이 일어났고, 헉슬리, 후커 등의 학자들이 다윈의 견해를 적극 지지하며, 반대자들과 논쟁을 벌였습니다.

그 결과 〈종의 기원〉은 세계 각국으로 출판되었고, 점차 다윈의 견해가 인정을 받게 되었습니다. 일흔이 넘는 나이에도 활발한 저술 활동을 하던 다윈은 1882년 병으로 자신의 집에서 생을 마감합니다. 다윈의 진화론은 사상의 혁신을 가져왔으며, 인류의 자연관, 세계관 형성에 많은 영향을 끼쳤습니다.

이 책을 만든 사람들

글 · 안형모

어린이들의 꿈을 키워 주는 재미있고 유익한 만화를 만들기 위해 즐겁게 작업하고 있습니다. 인물 이야기를 통해 위인들의 성공적인 업적보다는 성공에 이르기까지 과정과 노력을 담기 위해 노력합니다. 『천추태후』, 『통째로 한국사 1, 2』, 『호동왕자와 낭랑공주』 등의 만화 시나리오를 썼습니다.

그림 · 스튜디오 청비

기발한 상상력을 바탕으로 새롭고 재미있는 콘텐츠를 만들어 내는 만화 창작 집단입니다. 어린이들이 책을 읽고 큰 꿈을 품기를 바라는 마음으로 즐겁게 작업하고 있습니다. 작품으로 『성철 스님』, 『아 다르고 어 다른 우리말 101가지』, 『반기문 유엔 사무총장의 꿈과 도전』 등이 있습니다.

번역 · 채드 워커 (Chad Walker)

미국 텍사스 오스틴에서 심리학과 일본어를 전공했습니다. 일본으로 건너가 10년 간 살았고 이후 한국과 중국을 오가며 한 · 중 · 일의 동아시아 문화를 비교 연구하고 있습니다. 현재는 연세대학교 국어국문학과 박사 과정 중에 있습니다. 옮긴 책으로 『한국어 교육을 위한 한국어 연어사전』, 『한국인의 가치 문화』, 『속성 한국어』 등이 있습니다.

감수 · 김수희

연세대학교에서 역사를 전공했습니다. 이후 한국뿐 아니라 일본, 미국에서 한국어, 일본어, 영어를 가르쳐 왔으며 부모를 위한 영어교육용 책을 썼습니다. 영어교육채널 EBSe '엄마표 영어특강'에서 강의를 하며 홈스쿨, 알파벳과 파닉스, 다차원 테마 영어 수업 기법을 알리고 있습니다. 전국 각지에서 어린이 영어 교육에 대한 강연을 하며 창의적이고 열정적인 교수법으로 영어를 배우고자 하는 어린이와 부모들에게 많은 도움을 주고 있습니다.

Charles Darwin

While Darwin was on his voyage on the Beagle ship, where did he see giant tortoises and iguanas?

a. the Galapagos Islands
b. Hawaii
c. the South Pole

Answer: a

Contents

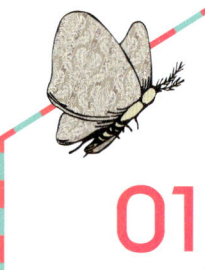

01 A Boy Full of Curiosity

Oh, a bee!

Gotcha!

Charles Robert Darwin was born into a wealthy physician's family on February 12, 1809 in Shrewsbury, England.

Mommy!

Darwin was the fifth of six children and had three older sisters, one older brother and one younger sister.

Oh…

As the daughter of Josiah Wedgwood, founder of the famous Wedgwood pottery company, Darwin's mother Susannah was also born into a wealthy family.

When Darwin was eight years old, his mother died after a battle with cancer.

From now on, Marianne and Caroline will assume your mother's role.

You two have to assume responsibility for looking after your brothers and sisters.

Yes, Father.

If they don't behave, then use the whip to punish them.

14

Charles' father, Robert Darwin, was a very sympathetic man with a keen intuition.

I wonder why Charles likes to wander about outside so much?

A respectable physician, he began treating patients around the age of 21 and was very successful at it.

He has no interest in studying and cares about nothing other than hunting around for rodents. This is serious.

I'm only taking one! He-he.

Oh, Father!

Why did you take just one bird egg?

I felt sorry for the birds. Besides, I only need one anyway.

Charles.

You don't find your schoolwork interesting?

Nope, I like to watch nature, collect shells and rocks and go fishing.

Nobody else in our family likes those kinds of things, so I wonder where such an interest came from?

From next year on, you will attend Dr. Butler's boarding school.

Huh?

School is not just a place to study. There are many other things to learn.

17

18

At the age of nine, Darwin entered Dr. Butler's boarding school in Shrewsbury.

Do you know what my favorite saying is?

Yes, it's "Don't be friends with someone you don't respect." Right?

Right. Now this is a good school, so you should study hard and make lots of friends.

Although his father liked the school, Dr. Butler's school was not a good match for the ever-inquisitive Darwin.

Yawn.

At the very rigid and strict school, most of his classes were nothing but ancient history and geography.

Darwin preferred observing nature more than studying and he spent most of his time out collecting rocks, observing insects or hunting down birds.

Charles, what's that book you're reading?

It's called The Natural History of Selborne and it describes nature observations conducted in Selborne. It's got great records of the habits of birds.

I thought you were only interested in insects and plants, but now birds too!

You're the first person I've ever met to have such a unique hobby.

When I went to Wales I noticed so many insects and bugs. It would have been nice if we had gone together.

Wales?

Well, yeah, um… Hee-hee.

21

*Heteroptera : A large group of about 40,000 species of insects in the Order Hemiptera.

22

24

The theory of evolution that Charles Darwin would later propose was not the first of its kind.

Wow, so all creatures came from shellfish?

Darwin's grandfather Erasmus also wrote a book related to the theory of evolution, *Zoonomia*.

I can't believe he wrote such an interesting book.

Even though the research Darwin would do later in life was very different from his thoughts during this time, it was his grandfather's book that would plant the seed for his concept of evolution.

If only Grandpa was still around, I could listen to many interesting stories.

Eek!

26

Darwin's father, concerned about his future, decided that Darwin quit the Shrewsbury boarding school and that he would personally train him to be a doctor.

How much longer are you going to perform chemistry experiments? Come and help me care for my patients.

Okay.

After leaving school, Darwin looked after poor patients as well as women and children while studying to be a doctor.

Please describe your symptoms in detail.

I have a cough and fever and no energy.

Then, that fall, he began formal medical training with his brother at Edinburgh University in Scotland.

I thought you'd be lonely.

Actually, I came to look after you!

However, Darwin soon learned he did not enjoy studying medicine.

Why did you change to this school?

Doctor, please let my son live!

What are you doing standing around? Quick, prepare for surgery!

It hurts so bad! Ow!

Pain medicine called anesthesia did not yet exist so surgery was performed while patients writhed and yelled in pain.

Ow!

I can't believe he's operating so fast!

He definitely is a doctor!

Wah!

I can't stand the sight of blood.

I don't think I'm cut out for this.

Both times Darwin performed surgery at school, he had to run out before it was completed because he couldn't bear the experience. He never attended another surgery class again.

The surgery isn't even over yet!

Charles! Where are you going?

Afterward, apart from Professor Thomas Hope's chemistry class, Darwin lost all interest in the medical classes at Edinburgh University.

02 A Biology Expert in Cambridge

 Track 11 ▶

Having lost his interest in studying at school, Darwin devoted himself to exploring the coast of Scotland and collecting oceanic life.

Grrrr!

Ahh!

Don't scare me like that!

Hahaha!

You've stitched the skin together too loosely.

Oh?

See, I knew you were doing it wrong.

Hmmph. I did alright.

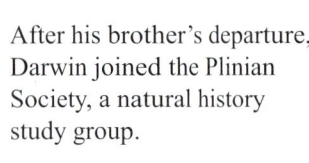

After his brother's departure, Darwin joined the Plinian Society, a natural history study group.

The study group gave Darwin opportunities to meet new friends, including William Ainsworth, Professor John Coldstream and Professor Robert Grant.

In particular, he attended the marine biology classes of Professors Coldstream and Grant, who would go to collect animals for dissection that lived in muddy beach areas.

Charles! Why don't you dissect this?

Eek!

Why do I have to do it?

Because there are already so many things here to dissect.

I never said I studied anatomy!

It appears he is not very fond of anatomy.

Ha ha ha!

Darwin was also very interested in geology and he attended a course taught by the authority on geology, Dr. Robert Jameson.

Now… what we saw outside was, that… almond-shaped molten rock and…

Yawn…

Professor Jameson's lectures are so boring.

But the Professor's geology museum is really cool!

Professor Jameson was in charge of the museum geological specimens and Darwin spent much time there stuffing birds for display.

Wow! Did you stuff all the birds in the museum? You should try dissection with the same zeal.

Hmm, I think I'd rather stuff off that mouth!

In April of 1827, Darwin left Edinburgh University after only two years and without earning a degree.

 **Track 13** ▶

After leaving Edinburgh, Darwin traveled around France for a few months.

Upon returning from France, Darwin went to Shropshire where he enjoyed hunting.

I got that last one.

Yep, I saw it with my own eyes!

Huh?

I don't get it. I was the one who shot the bird, but he keeps insisting that he did.

Don't worry, you've got your witness right here.

Really?

Darwin remained in Shropshire for a while and became acquainted with Fanny Owen, the daughter of a prestigious family.

Around this time, Darwin's father learned that Darwin did not want to become a doctor.

Charles is spending all his time traveling and hunting.

At this rate, he'll end up being a lazy good-for-nothing.

Does it hurt when I press here?

Yes.

Charles says he has no intention whatsoever of becoming a doctor.

What!

Have Charles return home at once!

Yes, Father.

CRAAAK

Ow!

At the time, to become a clergyman you had to have a degree from a university in England.

I'm not devout enough to become a member of the clergy, but if that's Father's wish, then I guess I have no choice.

You made it. Who would have thought we'd meet again so soon, ha ha.

Darwin had not studied any classical literature since middle school, but after studying with a private tutor, he was able to enter Cambridge University's Christ's College in January 1828.

Brother!

I don't think I would really fit in with that crowd anyway.

This is our second cousin, William Darwin Fox.

Long time no see, Charles.

Yeah.

So you'll probably need a lot of money if you plan to join their hunting parties.

There are about 2,000 students living here at Cambridge and most of them are children of the most prestigious families in England.

Don't worry, Charles is perfectly happy chasing after bugs by himself.

Oh?

Great. That means you've come to the right place, Charles.

What?

This is the house of Reverend Henslow, a botany professor. He always welcomes any student who has an interest in natural history.

Oh, Professor Henslow!

I've heard a lot about him. He apparently has a vast knowledge of entomology, chemistry, mineralogy and geology.

You're right.

That's Professor Henslow over there.

Ah…

Darwin's older cousin, William Darwin, introduced him to Professor Henslow, who would have a big impact on Darwin's life.

This is my cousin, Charles Darwin, whom I told you about.

Please make yourself at home. I can sense that you are quite fond of nature.

Pardon?

Due to their common interest in nature and biology, Darwin and Professor Henslow were able to discuss many things and soon became quite close.

But Professor! You said the same things about us too!

Do you think everyone values nature the same? You all see nature in terms of cattle sheds, but Charles sees nature in terms of flowers.

Charles spent approximately half of his time at Cambridge University taking walks with Professor Henslow.

So, does that mean we smell like cow manure?

No, no, not quite that serious!

HA HA HA

40

42

Charles! I caught a Crucifix Ground Beetle!

Really?

Here, it's yours.

Thanks, William!

Consider it a good-bye gift from me. I'll be graduating soon.

What?

First my brother leaves and now you?

After both his brother and cousin William passed their final exams and left the university, Darwin suddenly became very lonely.

For some time afterward, Darwin lost his sense of purpose and was feeling low. He began meeting up with friends, staying out late and neglecting his coursework. As a result, his grades suffered greatly.

Today, let's just forget about school and have some fun!

Great idea, Charles!

Darwin spent his summer vacation collecting ground beetles and reading. In the winter, he went hunting with Fanny.

It's been great until now, but I'll probably be bored from now on given that both my brother and George have left.

How's school going?

So you were just fine without me. I see.

What are you talking about?

Charles, I'm seeing someone else.

I can't believe it!

I'm so sorry, Charles.

As usual, Darwin's father was not pleased with his progress.

You call these grades? You think you have a chance at becoming a clergyman with marks like this?

Darwin had serious arguments with his father about his bad grades.

Yes, Father, but all I need to do is make sure I graduate.

What!

Moreover, after Darwin received word that Fanny had become engaged to another man, he made up his mind to pour all his energy into studying.

That's it. From now on, I will do nothing but study.

Darwin went on to receive his bachelor's degree, ranking 10th in his class.

Congratulations! I thought you couldn't do it!

And I thought he'd end up becoming an insect trader.

Hey, are you congratulating or insulting me!

However, because he had originally entered Cambridge University on probationary status, he had to enroll in two additional semesters of classes even after passing his final exams.

Darwin, you know you still have to attend school for two semesters, right?

Yes, Sir.

It was then that Professor Henslow recommended to Darwin that he study geology.

This would be good for me too.

You mean I don't have to attend school anymore?

I mean, if you have to attend school anyway, then why not study geology?

So how is that good?

Professor Sedgwick is heading to North Wales on a field trip to research old rock formations. I'll put in a good word for you and see if you can join him.

Really?

Ha ha ha!

I knew you'd be interested.

Darwin joined Professor Sedgwick on his geology investigation to North Wales, visiting areas including Llangollen, Conway, Bangor and Capel Curig.

Come along with me. You can collect the rock samples and mark the geological layers on the map.

Yes, Professor.

Like this?

Yes, great job!

Take a look. There might even be fossils inside.

Fossils!

*Naturalist : A scholar of natural history, which is the study of the types, attributes, distribution and habitats of plants and animals.

03 The Voyage of the Beagle

 Track 21 ▶

Being included as a naturalist on the voyage of the Beagle would prove to be a life-changing event for Darwin. Darwin decided to accept Professor Henslow's invitation.

However, he ran into opposition from one person whose strong support he needed most-- his father.

You want to take a trip for two years?

No, absolutely not.

But it's not just to travel.

I'll be going as a naturalist on a British navy survey ship.

That's even more questionable!

And they plan to take you along, with no credentials as a naturalist whatsoever? Sounds very suspicious to me.

Oh boy…

I'm sure my judgment is sound. However...

There's surely nobody that Father knows who would agree to this.

If there was even one person whom I considered an authority to advise you to get on that ship, then I would agree to your plan.

51

Darwin replied to Professor Henslow declining his offer to join the Beagle expedition. To help himself deal with his sadness, he went hunting with his cousins.

On this hunting trip, however, he happened to meet his uncle Josiah, who supported Darwin.

Don't worry. I'll do my best to persuade your father to let you go.

Really?

Together, they wrote a letter to Darwin's father in hopes of changing his mind.

Dear Mr. Darwin,

To My Esteemed Father,

Darwin's father read the letters and finally agreed to allow Darwin to go aboard the Beagle.

If a rational person like Josiah Wedgwood agrees with this plan, I see no reason to object.

At this point, Darwin could not even imagine that the planned trip of two years would continue for nearly five.

We're finally on our way.

There were 74 crew members, including a doctor, painter, furniture maker and carpenter, along with 6 deckhands, aboard the Beagle.

Some of you are on a ship for the first time, so please help each other.

Yes, Sir!

Darwin?

Are you okay?

You'll probably feel lonely for a while.

Gulp!

10 days after departing from Devonport, England, the Beagle arrived at Tenerife Island.

Land ahoy!

However, due to rumors among the inhabitants of infectious diseases spreading from England, the crew was not allowed to go ashore.

Sorry, but we cannot allow you to leave the ship.

What should we do?

If there are diseases we must stay on board.

The next morning, when Darwin saw the rising sun illuminate Tenerife peak through the clouds, he was overwhelmed with emotion.

We depart at first light tomorrow.

Yes, sir.

Ah!

The Beagle continued its voyage, dropping anchor next at the Cape Verde Islands off the west coast of Africa.

What… what's that?

Isn't it just a bunch of barren lava rocks?

The ground here must have become inhospitable to life due to the heat of the tropical sun and volcanic eruptions.

But being able to find palm trees in such a desolate place is still quite amazing.

Indeed.

Oh! That bird caught a lizard!

That's an Indian kingfisher!

That bird may not be as beautiful as the Indian kingfishers in England, but it seems quite swift.

Wow, you really do know a lot!

Hey, why is the sky so hazy?

Oh!

It's fine dust. Looks like it has blown over from Africa.

Huh?

You mean dust can blow all this way from the mainland?

Sure can, easily.

This must be the same phenomenon that explains how seeds of flowerless plants are spread across wide areas.

?

No matter the topic, he always ends up talking about insects and plants.

Oh! There's an octopus!

Sure is!

After finding octopi on the island of St. Jago in the Cape Verde Islands, Darwin made repeated observations of their attributes.

I bet if we cooked it, it would taste delicious!

Wow, it tries to escape while freely moving and changing all parts of its body.

Now where do you think you're going!

What's this?

Ha ha!

Splaat!

64

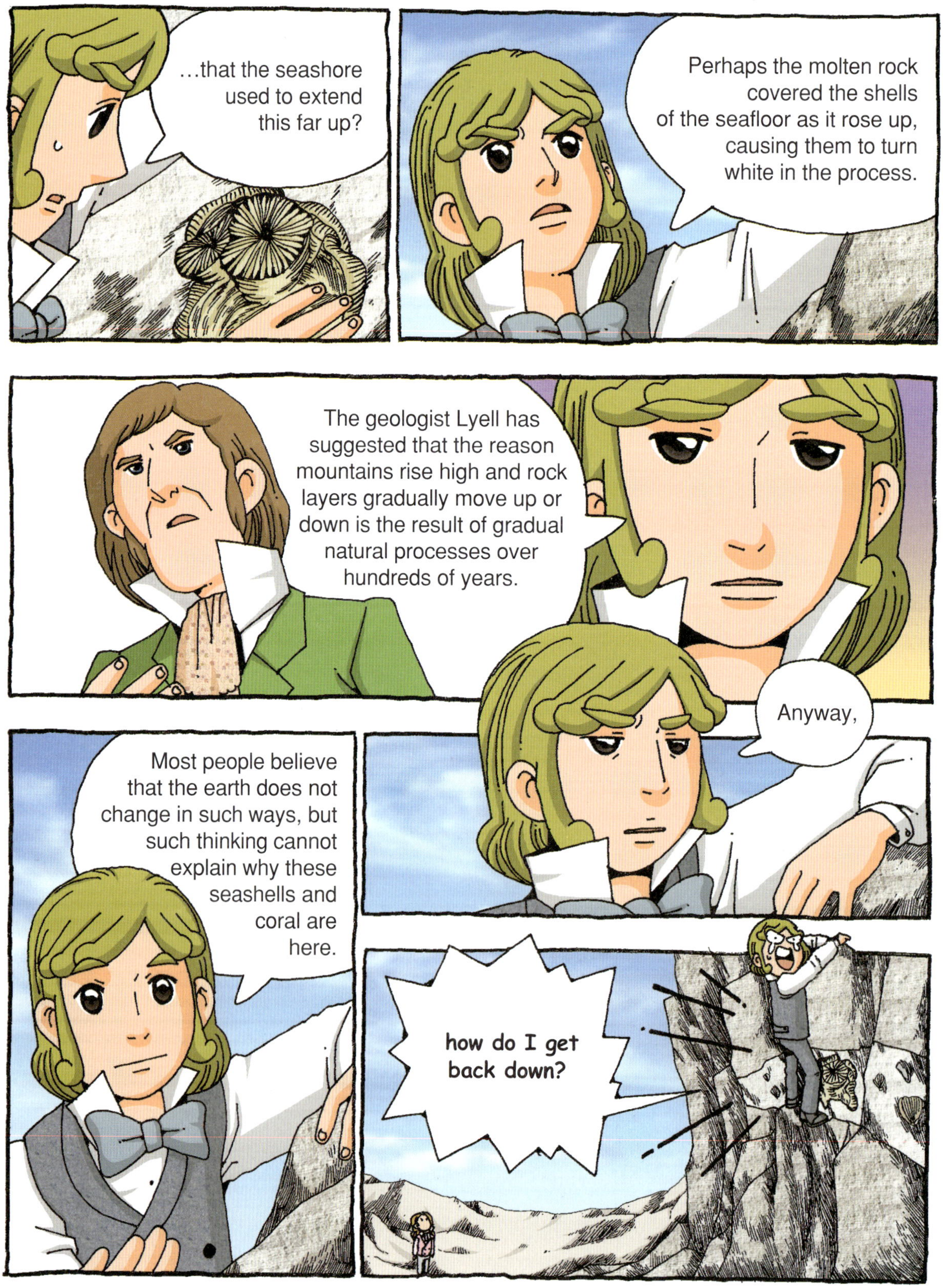

…that the seashore used to extend this far up?

Perhaps the molten rock covered the shells of the seafloor as it rose up, causing them to turn white in the process.

The geologist Lyell has suggested that the reason mountains rise high and rock layers gradually move up or down is the result of gradual natural processes over hundreds of years.

Anyway,

Most people believe that the earth does not change in such ways, but such thinking cannot explain why these seashells and coral are here.

how do I get back down?

66

The Beagle did not stay at the Cape Verde Islands for very long.
It set sail again and headed across the Atlantic Ocean toward Brazil.

Reading more geology books?

Yes, the evidence of changes in the earth that I've witnessed so far strongly support the claims of Lyell.

Pardon?

Charles is more tenacious and attentive than he might first appear.

Once something grabs his attention he dives right into it with great curiosity.

It's time to learn some traditional nautical knowledge.

Everyone who is crossing the equator for the first time has to participate.

Sir?

Dressed up as Poseidon, mythical god of the sea, Captain FitzRoy taught awareness of the effects of the equator.

Throw him in!

Oh!

SPLASH

The Beagle continued on its voyage, arriving in Bahia (modern-day Salvador), Brazil.

Wow! I've never seen such a lush jungle.

There are sure to be many different kinds of insects and birds.

70

I've got to make the insects I've captured into specimens and send them to Professor Henslow.

Professor, I'm having a fantastic time here. Following the paths of fluttering butterflies, I have discovered countless rare trees.

I can't describe words the incredible things I have witnessed as a naturalist walking through the Brazilian forest.

Inside the jungles of Brazil, Darwin realized his purpose in life.

My destiny is to become a scholar of nature.

After the crew completed its tasks at Bahia, the Beagle departed for Rio de Janeiro, the capital of Brazil at the time.

72

No food for the slaves who are lazy!

That man has crossed the line.

Slaves are people too! How can you treat them that way?

TAP

That's enough. You'll get hurt.

He bought those slaves with his own money, so others have no right to interfere.

That's rubbish!

I think the practice of slavery is wrong.

I think they should be able to live free lives.

I don't think you understand. Slaves are living better lives here than they would be in Africa.

I once visited a farm and the owner there asked his slaves if they would rather be free. All of them answered "No".

What else are they going to say in front of their master?

If they had answered honestly, they would surely have been whipped.

So what are you saying?

I won't hear any more of this. Don't even think about speaking to me again.

I just think your position on slavery should change.

What?

Darwin departed for Cape Frio along with six others.

I should be able to collect lots of plants and insects during this trip to Cape Frio.

I'm on my way home after participating in a festival, so it's great having a companion on the way back.

I doubt you'll ever be bored as long as I'm around. Ha ha!

A firefly!

It's amazing how they glow.

These are Western fireflies. When stimulated, they glow very bright, but then, after some time has passed, the rings around their bodies begin to dim.

They emit light from two rings simultaneously, but the glow from the front part seems more powerful.

The substance that glows is a very sticky liquid.

The light continues to flow out of the parts where the skin was torn, while those parts where there was no injury remain dim.

Even after removing the insect's head from the body, the rings continue to glow, but the intensity is not as strong as before.

And if I poke its body in various places with a needle, it emits a brighter glow.

It seems that fireflies only have the ability to conceal or extinguish their glow momentarily, and otherwise have no control over it.

Yaaaawwnn!

Zzzzzz…

!

Looks like I thoroughly bored him.

Darwin made detailed observations of the habitats, characteristics and behavior of the local invertebrate animals.

Wow, living things also live inside rotten logs.

And at a lake along the coastline he observed snails and *bivalves having both freshwater and saltwater characteristics.

Even after they've died, their shells seem to keep living.

He discovered that creatures of the same family, even if they lived in geographically separated areas, had similar traits.

Does this mean that all members of the same family have the same characteristics?

*Bivalves : Mollusks with two-part, symmetrical shells.

He also observed various characteristics of local spiders, including how they hunted prey, their situation-specific behavior patterns, and the shapes of their webs.

......

So this is how spiders hunt their prey.

You truly are a keen observer, very befitting a naturalist aboard the Beagle.

Hey, what's this?

It's a poisonous spider!

A p-p- poisonous spider?

......

Yikes!!

CRASH

The farm to which Darwin was invited was a large estate with a large number of slaves.

I'll sell off all the women who don't work!

It was very distressing for Darwin to see slaves experience such cruel, sub-human treatment.

I see now how both my father's and grandfather's opposition to slavery was fitting.

I can't stand to witness this anymore. I shall head back to the ship and prepare to return to England.

My explosive temper caused me to say some terrible things to Charles.

I'll leave the ship just as soon as I can pack my things.

And just where do you plan on going?

You ordered me to leave.

If you leave the ship, who will I have to talk to?

Captain!

Charles, I apologize for being so rude to you.

Darwin learned from this experience that even though some topics may be hard to talk about, it is better to express how you feel, as opinionsare valued.

You were worried about my having to go back to England by myself, weren't you?

The next time you talk back to me like that, I'll have you walk the plank!

Even after Darwin became a world-renowned doctor years later, he would always choose his words carefully before discussing sensitive political issues.

Everyone has a different opinion. Even if I disagree with it, I should still be respectful.

Sir! You got a letter from England!

A letter?

It's from sister Caroline.

82

Charles.

Professor!

I've decided to return to England.

What?

Without the Beagle's official naturalist how will we complete our nature surveys?

Well, they've still got you, haven't they? You've got more passion and much more ability than I.

Professor.

I'm naming you naturalist on this voyage.

With the departure of the Professor, Darwin became the new official naturalist of the Beagle.

I have a lot more responsibility now.

On July 5, 1832, the Beagle set sail for Buenos Aires.

04 The Birth of the Theory of Evolution

CD1 Track 38 ▶

Darwin sent the samples he had collected while on the Beagle to Professor Henslow.

Ah, Charles has sent me more samples and stuffed specimens.

He did a fine job collecting various animals and insects, and his results are well organized.

I'll have to present his research findings in his place.

They say a guy named Darwin has made some surprising discoveries.

He's someone to keep an eye out for in the future.

For the next two years the ship sailed along the eastern coast south of the Plata River, and the southern tip of South America.

We will be surveying this area for the time being. Everyone is responsible for fulfilling their assigned duties.

Darwin remained in Maldonado for 10 weeks, and kept busy shooting and creating new specimens.

POW

This place is completely different from the jungle. We should be able to collect lots of new animals here.

Just leave it to me! I'll do anything! Hee-hee.

Why did you bring me along?

I'll need you to help me out. I can pay you.

Pay!

86

The Beagle spent two years traveling up and down the coast of Argentina to make more precise nautical maps.

After reaching Tierra del Fuego at the southern tip of South America, the Beagle returned to Buenos Aries, and then made a trip to the Falkland Islands.

Be sure there are no errors in your measurements.

Yes, sir.

While the Beagle was out on cartographical survey trips, Darwin was doing his own exploring of the surrounding areas.

I thought we might get to rest some today.

No, today we're heading to Punta Alta, a really interesting place.

Here, Darwin found a huge fossil as large as an elephant.

It looks like a fossil.

These aren't the bones of any animal currently living in South America.

89

Darwin worried that Henslow might ridicule his efforts.

What if I send this and really do become a laughingstock?

However, contrary to Darwin's fears, the European scientists who saw the fossils he sent took them very seriously, causing a huge commotion in the scientific community.

Wow, this is a fossil of the giant sloth, or Megatherium.

It looks like an armadillo fossil to me.

And just think, we thought we'd found all the giant, elephant-sized animals.

With these fossils, Darwin is researching how animals change over the passage of time.

For example, the relationship between the current day sloth and the armadillos of the past.

92

I shot a bird!

Yep, and thanks to you I will be able to examine even more animals.

Let's go to Pampas tomorrow.

Okay!

I'll have to show off my shooting skills to everyone there! Heh-heh!

Darwin often went to the Pampas plains in southern Argentina.

Yahoo!

He rode horses with South American cowboys, called gauchos, and helped teach them how to make a living.

I was great yesterday, but I don't know what's happened today.

So when exactly are you going to show us what you can do?

The natives stole our smaller boats, and in an effort to negotiate to get them back we took some natives hostage.

However, the natives ran away and the negotiations fell through.
But there was one young native girl that didn't run away, asking if she could instead stay behind with us on the Beagle.

That's a fine idea.

Since our mission was to spread civilization, we decided to use the girl in an experiment.

What kind of experiment?

We would take a few of the natives back to England with us and attempt to civilize them.

Then, we would return them to their native land with hopes that they could civilize the rest of their tribe.

Oh!

The Beagle arrived at Tierra del Fuego, South America.

We'll need to build a temporary camp.

Yes sir, Captain!

After the crew had set up camp, the natives along with a missionary left the ship and then the Beagle departed to continue exploring.

After the Beagle returned nine days later, the crew was shocked to hear what had happened during their absence.

As soon as you left, the natives stole all my things and attacked the camp.

I defended the camp the best I could for the first few days, but in the end they stole everything.

Unbelievable!

I guess it's not possible for only a few people to change everyone after all.

You all stay here and start a new life.

Yes, sir.

Let's go, there's nothing more we can do here.

Before long, the natives who had been educated in England returned to their previous lifestyle. FitzRoy's experiment had been an utter failure.

I had hoped there would be a positive result.

On June 10, 1834, after traveling around the Atlantic Ocean for two years, the Beagle turned its sails toward the Pacific Ocean.

Finally, the Pacific Ocean!

We're finally escaping the cursed Atlantic!

The original plan of a two-year voyage has become quite extended.

If there's anyone who wants to go home, just let me know anytime.

What about you?

I'll stay with the Beagle until the completion of its mission.

Oh, really?

If I say I want to go back to England early, the captain is certain to be displeased.

Ah, I see the Captain has been moved by my enthusiastic sense of loyalty.

Why isn't he choosing to go home? He has to get off the boat before all his stuff can be cleaned up.

More than anything, I can't afford to discontinue my nature observations. I've got to confirm what kinds of insects, plants, and animals live in the Pacific Ocean.

I had no idea Chile has such refined cities.

It's like we're in Paris.

The Beagle followed the coast of Chile and arrived in Valparaiso.

We'll be staying here for a while.

Where do you plan to stay overnight?

I have a friend from back home.

So I plan to go stay with him.

Darwin visited the house of his hometown friend he hadn't seen since his childhood, Richard Corfield.

Charles! How many years has it been?

It feels like a dream getting to meet you here on the other side of the world!

I can't believe that troublemaker Charles has become the naturalist for a Royal Navy survey ship.

I simply focused on collecting insects and plants. I was never the troublemaker you were.

Indeed, I thought you might even turn into an insect yourself!

I see, ha ha!

After leaving his friend's house, Darwin followed the west coast of South America to study the geology of the Andes Mountains.

Take care!

Thank, I'll stop by again on my way back.

105

As September approached, Darwin traveled around Chile, becoming fascinated with its beautiful scenery and enjoying fine dining.

Feel free to come and stay with me anytime.

You're so lucky to be living here.

Aaagghh!

Charles, what's wrong?

My stomach, it hurts really bad.

Oh dear! You must have an upset stomach. I'll get you back to my place and call a doctor.

Some bad wine was the cause of Darwin's illness. He stayed in bed for one month at his friend's house.

I'm sorry for causing such a burden.

You were always welcome here anyway, so no need to feel that way.

106

Beagle Captain FitzRoy was on the verge of bankruptcy after trying to purchase a boat for personal needs.

I've come so far and have gone through so much, and they won't even let me buy a small boat?

Upset with the Admiralty for refusing his funding request, Captain FitzRoy became enraged.

I'm resigning immediately!

Calm down, Captain!

The crew believes in you, Captain. If you resign, what will they do?

And I mean All of us!

Somehow we all have to get back to England.

You're right, it looks like I got a little too upset.

Prepare to finish the survey work and then return to England.

We're so happy to hear you say that, Captain.

Yeah!

Captain, you're the best!

As soon as the Beagle arrived in Chile, the fully recovered Darwin joined them.

From the deck of the Beagle, Darwin intently observed a volcanic eruption.

The power of nature is truly incredible.

In February, 1835, after completing its survey duties along the southern Chilean coast, the Beagle stopped briefly at the port of Valdivia.

Of course we can't skip the chance to collect insects here as well.

Couldn't we rest a bit first?

Here, Darwin experienced an earthquake for the first time. It jolted the ground and destroyed buildings.

The ground! What's happening?

RUUUMMBLE

This must be what they call an earthquake.

Earthquake?

The earth really shook! It really shook!

The two-minute long earthquake left the city in shambles.

I had no idea an earthquake could cause this much damage.

The crew of the Beagle helped in the reconstruction of the city. In the process, Darwin discovered a place where the earth's surface had risen slightly due to the earthquake.

Here's a slab of rock mixed with mussel shells.

This must have been pushed up above sea level by the earthquake.

Yes, that's it!

Over the course of hundreds of years and thousands of earthquakes, the earth's surface was raised up to form what we see today, and this must have been how the fossils I saw in the Andes Mountains formed.

Here's a petrified tree!

This is further evidence of large-scale geologic change.

At the beginning of April Darwin returned to Mr. Corfield's house to record his new discoveries. He also wrote a long letter to Professor Henslow explaining his findings, and sent it along with some collected specimens.

Professor Henslow should enjoy hearing about these new discoveries.

I'm impressed by your devotion.

With Darwin on board again, the Beagle set off north for Peru.

However, a revolution had just broken out in Peru, preventing them from docking there. As a result, The Beagle left the coast of South America and headed for the Pacific Ocean.

The Beagle arrived at its first destination in the Pacific Ocean, the Galapagos Islands.

05 The Galapagos Islands

The Galapagos Islands are a group of islands with an unusually large amount of hardened black lava rocks. Most of the animals living on the islands seemed to be lizards and birds, so Darwin didn't expect to find much when he began his exploration.

Ho-hum.

What are those hideous things?

There's an iguana, lizard, and a giant tortoise…

Very scary looking.

These animals are a good match for the dull surroundings.

That's the first time I've ever heard you react like that.

Darwin didn't feel that the Galapagos Island were anything special.

What, you think I fall in love with every place I see for the first time?

There are also places I don't quite fancy.

Although the fact that there seemed to be only lizards and birds on the islands was one reason for Darwin's displeasure, the main reason was that he had been misinformed about the Galapagos.

There's nothing more than a few types of flowers and some common birds here.

Even then, the habitat of the rare animals that lived on the Galapagos was not correctly understood. It was thought that the giant tortoises came from the Indian Ocean and the iguanas from South America.

There's no point in studying animals that aren't even in their own habitats.

116

117

119

I wonder how recently the molten rock cooled and hardened. It's as hard as iron.

Judging from the fact that there's not much mud accumulated, the lava must have risen up to form the islands relatively recently.

Hmm? Who could those people be?

Allow me to introduce the acting Governor of the Galapagos.

Oh.

I'm the Beagle's naturalist, Charles Darwin.

I welcome you to the Galapagos, ha ha!

I myself am quite interested in the study of nature. I can look at a tortoise shell and tell exactly from which island it came.

What? By looking at its shell alone?

Darwin would find a clue to evolution in this single statement.

The tortoise shells are different from island to island?

Darwin belatedly realized that even birds living on the various islands of the Galapagos differed slightly in appearance depending on which island they inhabited.

Now why would the animals have different appearances if they lived in similar climates and at the same altitude?

It's no special discovery or anything. I had no idea you'd be so surprised. Ha ha!

You idiot!

! ! !

 Track 05 ▶

I can't believe it took me this long to realize such an important fact!

Did you just call me an idiot?

Gov-Governor, he wasn't directing that torward you.

Quick, there's no time. We've got to collect as much as we can!

Darwin's research on the Galapagos Islands had a major influence on his life because it was there that he came to understand the differences and similarities between creatures, forming the basis of his theory of evolution.

Until he began observing the animals on the Galapagos in detail, Darwin had believed that all the birds were the same as those 960 kilometers away in South America.

I've got to collect everything that would make a good specimen.

Anyone would have naturally come to such a conclusion...

Syms, get up!

…because it was generally believed that birds living on the South American continent would fly across to the islands and live there.

Come on, let's go hunting!

What's the occasion?

Darwin had even thought that all the various finches he had captured on different islands were different species, and thus had categorized them separately.

I'd better categorize them according to type so they'll be easy to identify.

Darwin carefully observed in what ways the birds and animals of the various islands differed.

Even birds from islands close together have differences.

What did they eat to become so heavy?

Oh!

That's it!
Maybe the birds' beaks changed depending on the food available on the island where they lived.

The birds living on each island adapted to their respective environments, changing little by little into different forms.

Birds that flew over to the Galapagos from the South American continent long ago adapted to the unique island ecosystems and remained here.

Then, over the passage of time, they evolved into slightly different species.

124

If I am correct…

…then this would have to apply to all animals in every ecosystem in the world.

In other words, all the world's species weren't created…

…they evolved gradually from earlier species.

Because the Galapagos Islands were isolated from other areas, they were perfect places to collect evidence for the theory.

There were not too many different species of creatures, and they rarely had any contact with other ecosystems.

Prepare the tortoises!

Yes, sir.

Huh? There were two here before. Where did they go?

Now that I look more closely, they really are different!

The Beagle departed the Galapagos Islands and began crossing the expansive Pacific Ocean.

We're finally heading back to England.

After stopping briefly in Tahiti, the Beagle continued on toward New Zealand.

The New Zealand Maori and the Tahitian natives seem to be similar races, but their personalities are very different.

I'd say the Tahitians are a little more sociable.

Leaving New Zealand, the Beagle continued on to Australia, where it cast anchor briefly.

Those guys are criminals that have been deported from England.

Really?

You mean they are all ex-convicts?

Shh! Quiet!

Darwin was greatly disheartened to find that sheep ranchers would indiscriminately kill wild animals.

I've had enough of this continent.

Leaving Australia behind, the Beagle next arrived at the Keeling Islands in the Indian Ocean.

Investigate the Indian Ocean coral reefs. This is your last duty of our journey.

127

Darwin spent a few days collecting coral reef samples so he could observe their structure under a microscope, and he also enjoyed observing tropical fish.

It's hard to tell whether coral is a plant or animal.

There's coral extending thousands of feet below the surface.

I see my theory is correct about coral growing on top of sunken islands.

The Beagle crossed the Indian Ocean and arrived in South Africa.
At ascension Island Darwin received a letter from his sister Catherine.

It's from catherine.

Professor Henslow collected all the letters you sent him and has published them as a book.

Oh my!

All the top scientists and upper-class intellectuals have read the book, which has made you quite the talk of the town.

......

Professor, you can't publish all of my writings for the whole world to see!

Sir, there's been a problem!

As soon as I see him we're gonna have to talk about this.

To double-check the longitudinal measurements we took previously the Captain says we have to go back to Brazil!

It can't be!

No, I can't stand being on the open sea any more!

KA-THUNK

After returning to Brazil once more and finishing all of its assigned orders, the Beagle braved stormy weather to finally arrive back in England on October 2, 1836.

It's been 4 years, 9 months, and 5 days since I left.

129

06 Evidence for Evolution

 Track 09 ▶

Ah, what a good night's sleep.

B-Burglar! Burglar!

Burglar? Where? Where is he?

You see, um, we couldn't really wash properly on the ship.

What?

Follow me! You're taking a bath right now!

OUCH!

I can wash myself. I'm an adult you know!

Ha ha ha!

Darwin was extremely busy for the first two years after returning home.

Boy, when will I ever have time to organize all this?

I've brought some professional assistants to help with your organization and research tasks.

He had to organize and catalog the materials and samples he sent to Professor Henslow during his voyage and others he brought back on the Beagle himself.

Professor Henslow!

132

Professor Henslow introduced Darwin to professionals in various fields who agreed to assist in categorizing his work.

This is Richard Owen, an animal anatomist.

I've heard so much about you.

I will examine the fossils.

Please let me be in charge of the birds.

Oh, you must be the ornithologist John Gould.

This one is part of my group, but I'm not sure where it needs to go.

I've rented a research laboratory at Cambridge University, so no need to worry about where to put things.

Darwin was approached by Captain FitzRoy about writing up his natural history discoveries as part of the official sea voyage report.

A record of the voyage of the Beagle?

Yes, with you writing the natural history portion.

To prepare a precise account of the journey I'll need the help of someone who can provide honest advice.

Most of the scientists available as consultants lived in London, and so did Darwin's brother Erasmus. He was soon on his way.

Brother!

Charles!

A sea voyage! You must no longer be the coward you used to be!

What? Coward?

Say that again and you'll be sorry!

Yikes!

Then I won't tell you that the geologist Lyell has returned from exploring the Amazon!

Is that true?

In London Darwin met his hero, the geologist, Charles Lyell.

I've respected you for so long, I feel as if we've known each other for decades.

Well, my features are common enough. Ha ha!

134

Thanks to your book *Principles of Geology*, I was deeply inspired during my voyage.

The pleasure is all mine, for you found proof of the theories I described in my book.

He's being very modest.

Darwin soon found his own place to live and moved out of his brother's house.

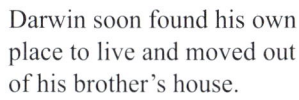

Thanks for everything, Brother.

You haven't seemed very well lately, so please take care of yourself.

There were many factories that burned coal in London, so the air was very polluted.

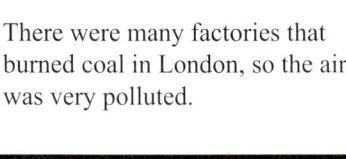

The London air is so bad, it's given me a headache.

But I have to stay here for the time being, so I have no other choice.

HACK, HACK

Meanwhile, the ornithologist Gould had discovered that the bird specimens Darwin brought from the Galapagos had been incorrectly categorized.

There was a mistake in the bird samples you made in the Galapagos.

Surely not!

In these samples, names were given based on the size of the beaks. However all of these birds are finches.

All of them are finches?

Yes. They are all slightly different in appearance, but they are all varieties of finches.

This discovery motivated Darwin to think more deeply about the concept of "species variation."

Does that mean one species can slowly change into another species?

Long ago, a flock of finches from South America likely got caught in a violent storm and ended up on the Galapagos Islands.

They then spread out among the islands, acquiring their own territory, and ended up staying there.

But the plants available for food existed in slightly different forms on each island.

Over time, the birds' beaks must have slowly changed to become more suitable for eating the available vegetation.

The fact that finches underwent such change is indisputable!

But what exactly was it that caused the finches' outer appearance to change?

No matter how you look at it, that sure looks a lot like an *armadillo.

What!

What did you just say? That this giant fossil really looks like an armadillo?

*Armadillo: A mammal about 40~70cm in length.

Yes. This fossil does not exist on the earth today, but it is very similar to smaller modern animals such as armadillos and sloths.

Animals that don't exist!

Today nobody is surprised to hear that animals changed gradually over time and according to their environments, but back in the 1800s it was a "crazy" idea.

The history of the earth is much longer than we had thought, and life has gradually evolved over time.

That's preposterous!

He's a radical revolutionary!

And he wants to overthrow the government!

All life was created at once by God.

It's not yet time to speak my ideas.

I've got to get all my thoughts together before I can properly publish the results of my research.

140

Darwin became a member of the Geological Society of London and presented numerous strong theories.

The South American continent is slowly rising.

He presented papers not only about the rising of the Andes Mountains, but also about other related subjects, such as his visit to an active volcanic region and his observations on the distribution of coral reefs.

I knew for certain after experiencing a major earthquake, for I had already discovered shell fossils at the mountain peaks.

Darwin was appointed secretary of the Geological Society, and was also elected to trustee of the Society.

Your talk about the Andes Mountains was good, but your theories about the coral reefs are excellent.

I thought coral reefs grew up around the craters of extinct volcanoes, but it looks like that isn't the case after all.

I started that research wondering if coral started growing around the shallow areas surrounding islands.

141

Darwin met Emma, who was visiting London, He was very attracted to her.

I hear you were on the Beguile for quite some time?

Ha ha! It wasn't the Beguile; it was the Beagle. Ha ha!

Darwin thought much about marriage, and especially about marriage to Emma Wedgwood.

The advantages and disadvantages of marriage:
Marriage causes you to become lazy and waste your valuable time. However, compared to raising a pet, getting married seems preferable.

No, no! Better than a pet! What am I thinking!

Spending my whole life alone will surely be lonely. I need a family.

At last, on January 29, 1839, Darwin married Emma Wedgwood

144

Darwin and Emma moved to the country town of Downe, on the outskirts of London.

Thanks for moving us out to the country.

Of course, it was your wish.

Actually, I wanted to move even more than you!

Around that time Darwin's book The Voyage of the Beagle was published.

Your book was incredibly interesting, especially the parts about the Andes Mountains and the Indian Ocean coral reefs.

What book is that?

It's Malthus' book on population.

Oh, you've been reading it too.

Because the rate of increase in food supply cannot keep up with the rate of human population increase, eventually only the strong survive… that's the best part of his theory.

Oh!

Darwin soon became completely engrossed in reading *Mathus' an Essay on the Principle of Population.*

I've been so frustrated about not ever figuring out the reason why the Galapagos finches underwent change, but this is the answer!

The answer lies in applying Mathus' population theory to all plants and animals.

All animals produce more offspring than will eventually survive.

If every animal born survived, the earth would soon be overflowing with animals. But most young animals die before becoming adults.

The offspring receive the fast legs of their mother.

That's it! Species variation happens through this process!

Darwin had a strong interest in professional animal breeders.

Breeders bred animals to carry the traits they wanted them to have.

Imagine crossing a gentle cat with a feisty dog, what do you think would be the result?

Well…

It's that kind of curiosity we deal with. We can create animals according to our customers' wishes.

Oh!

Looks like someone's had a selectively bred face.

Even this sort of artificial selection is similar to the process of change I've been thinking about.

But the process I'm thinking about is one in which humans don't interfere, a type of selection process that comes about naturally, a natural selection of sorts.

Indeed, from now on I'll call this theory "Natural Selection."

07 Animals That Survived

CD 2 Track 19 ▶

Honey!

CLANK

So-Sorry, these days I seem a bit weak.

Darwin was often sick after his time on the Beagle had ended.

Darwin suffered from shaking hands, headache, stomachache, insomnia, heart problems, vomiting, dermatitis, toothache, and had even fainted once.

Were you by chance bitten by a bug while at sea?

Not that I recall.

Very strange. I can't diagnose an illness that has your symptoms.

My mother was frail. Looks like I probably inherited this from her.

I still can't understand why the doctors can't figure out what's wrong.

Might it be psychological?

At that time medicine was not very advanced, and thus there was no doctor that could properly diagnose Darwin

Excessive stress and major life changes can also cause physical or mental symptoms.

In December 1839, Emma gave birth to their first son, William. Darwin was very proud to be a father.

This means I'm really a father now!

You did it, Emma!

Darwin was incredibly fond of his son, and they often played together.

Wawoo!

Zowie!

Soon, Darwin began making scientific observations of his son. He stored these notes for the time being, but later included them along with his observations of orangutans in a book he wrote.

He cries, and then the next moment he laughs. His range of emotion is amazing.

Kaff-Kaff

Darwin continued to write, with his health gradually becoming worse.

At age 32, Darwin was in great physical pain. It was even difficult for him to write. Nonetheless, he did not quit his research.

You need to stop working and rest a while, Honey.

But I want to further develop the coral reef research I performed while on the Beagle.

Something happened than, that excited Darwin.

Please come in, Hooker.

My friend!

A book had been published anonymously called *Vestiges of the Natural History of Creation*, and surprisingly it included content related to "transmutation of species".

Have you seen this book? I thought you might like it, so I brought you a copy.

The title alone has caught my eye.

No!

It only presents the problems with evolution. It doesn't provide any answer as to why humans and animals evolve!

The author's expertise in geology and zoology is elementary.

Either way, other scientists have been intensely critical of it.

Even Sedgwick went so far as to curse the thing.

Sedgwick did?

Even I could tell that whoever wrote it doesn't really know the definition of species.

Hooker was a young, 26 year-old botanist considered to be the top in his field. Darwin first met him when he enlisted help categorizing the specimens he had brought back from the Galapagos.

I also have written a book on transmutation of species. Without conclusive evidence, my book would probably be criticized by experts.

I've got to keep supplementing my work until I can discover more conclusive evidence.

Kaff-Kaff!

At this rate you're really going to injure your health.

In 1844, Darwin completed a more complete version of his book about transmutation of species, but its publication was postponed.

In case I die early, please take my writings and publish them as a book.

How can you talk like that?

Dear God!

I wonder what devout Christians like Emma think of my view that God didn't create all life on Earth?

155

In 1846, Darwin finally completed cataloguing all the specimens he had collected during his sea voyages.

It's finally finished! Going through all those collected samples was a great joy for me.

Huh? Looks like there's still one left.

Barnacles. They're so small they must have been overlooked.

Right, I need to thoroughly research these particular barnacles, the smallest species of all!

I've never seen such a perfectionist.

Darwin devoted eight years to the study of barnacles. His colleagues were surprised to find him so focused on this one specific topic.

They say he's already written four books on barnacles alone.

Then, on September 9, 1846, Darwin finally began categorizing all the records he had taken related to his theory of species.

It's now time to put the finishing touches on what I've researched thus far.

Darwin already knew how animals evolved when their environments changed.

In changing environments, only those animals that can adapt well can survive.

However, there was still one nagging question holding him back.

I still don't understand why there are fossils showing animals evolving even when the environment doesn't change.

How is this possible?

In 1854 Darwin found the answer to his question.

KLIK KLAK KLIK

That's it!

FLAP FLAP

Yes, it's rank!
To survive in nature, all life belongs to an *ecological hierarchy.

Let's suppose a species of monkey living in a forest. There are two types of fruit in the forest.

One grows on the top branches of the trees and is soft and sweet-tasting. The other fruit is on the ground, has a hard shell, and is tough to eat.

*Ecological hierarchy: The theory that two species of the same rank cannot coexist.

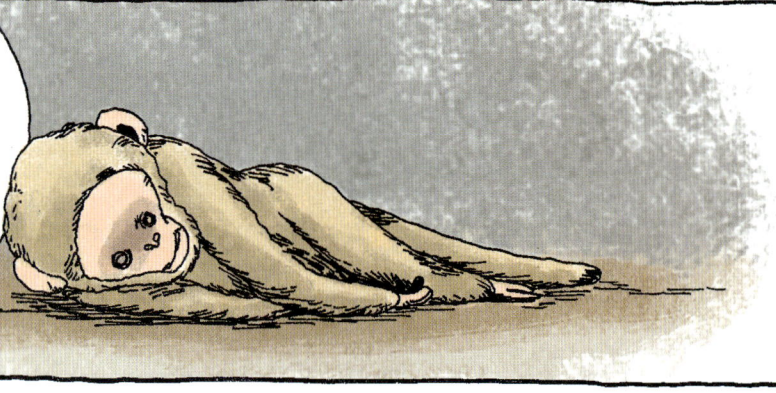

The normal monkeys can't pick the fruit from the trees or bite the fruit on the ground, so they gradually starve and die.

The surviving smaller monkeys breed other smaller monkeys, and eventually evolve into a smaller, more nimble variety of monkey.

This means that most of the original monkeys who had first come to the forest will become extinct.

Yes, that's it!

I've finally found the answer!

Darwin, unable to contain his enthusiasm, told those close to him of his theory.

I think it's a good theory, but you need to support it with some evidence.

I didn't care that much for that last theory, but this one is good.

Hmm, so just what part of what theory didn't you fancy?

No, I didn't mean it that way! Anyway, you better get those ideas down in a book before someone else steals your theory.

Darwin could not delay any longer. He poured all his energy into writing an account of his theory of natural selection based on the facts he had discovered first-hand.

Then, one day Darwin received astounding news.

Honey, you got a package from someone named Wallace.

Oh?

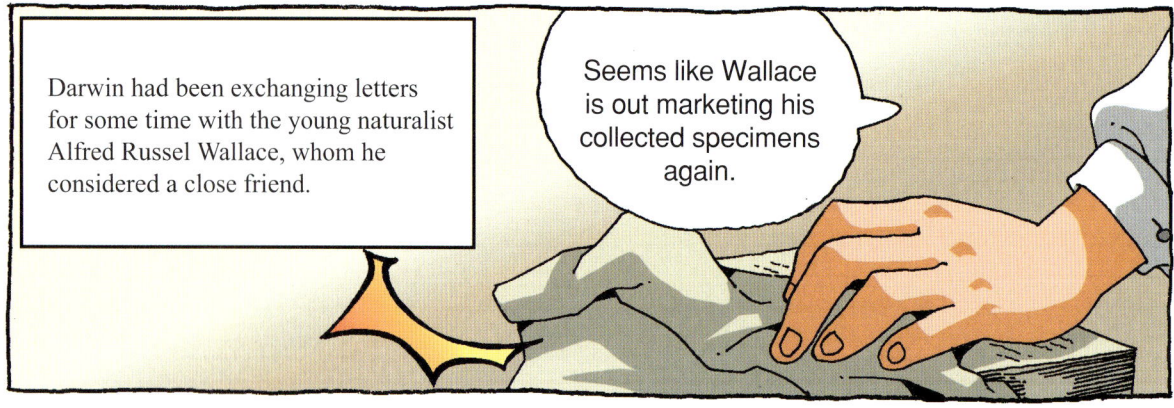

Darwin had been exchanging letters for some time with the young naturalist Alfred Russel Wallace, whom he considered a close friend.

Seems like Wallace is out marketing his collected specimens again.

Wallace was an explorer who traveled the world, and he often sent rare specimens he collected to English scientists in hopes they would purchase them.

Hmm? It looks like a research article. On the Tendency of Varieties to Depart Indefinitely From the Original Type…

Darwin was astonished by the article Wallace had sent him.

How can this be? Mutations, natural selection…

So there has been another scientist researching the same topics as me.

Wallace had also been researching the process of natural selection that Darwin had been pursuing for twenty years.

Oh my...

Now I won't be able to claim the theory of natural variation as my own discovery.

What have I been doing all this time? What good does it do to write a book now?

Darwin sent Wallace's paper and letter to Lyell. Lyell then told Hooker, and the three of them debated the issue together.

Can you believe the audacity of Wallace?

I know, basically he's written what has taken Charles 20 years to research and discover.

163

Lyell and Hooker decided to submit the paper as a joint presentation by both Darwin and Wallace to the *Linnean Society.

By presenting the paper jointly, both of them can get recognized.

Right, we've got to get Darwin to submit his findings as well.

Darwin sent letters he had exchanged with the American botanist Asa Gray and a paper he had written in 1844.

Professor, you're not going to attend the society?

We just had the funeral for my youngest son recently, so I'm afraid I won't be able to make it.

This will be how I present my paper on natural selection.

I wonder what the world's reaction will be to the publication of it?

The research is not completely finished yet, but it will surely prove to be shocking.

*Linnean Society: A scientific society for the study of taxonomy and natural history named after the Swedish naturalist Carolus Linnaeus.

In 1858, Lyell and Hooker together presented the work of Darwin and Wallace to the Linnean Society.

It turns out that life forms are not unchanging beings, as we have thought until now.

The variation of species for the purpose of natural selection...

Strange, contrary to our expectations, people don't seem very interested.

If Charles hears about this, he'll be devastated.

The theory of natural selection was received positively. Now that the contents of the theory are known, I suggest you finish your thesis without delay.

I'm so relieved to hear they received the theory of natural selection positively.

I've only written half the manuscript I'll have to hurry to finish it.

Darwin worked hard to finish his book on the theory of natural selection, including as many facts and types of evidence as he could.

In May 1859, Darwin completed his thesis, a total of 500 pages.

However, the thesis was so long that he decided to publish it as a book instead.

I'm worried that the book won't sell, and the publisher will lose money.

The content is sure to provoke controversy, so it should be popular.

Then, on November 24, 1859, the result of Darwin's lifetime of research, *The Origin of Species*, was finally published.

As soon as the book was released, all 1,250 copies of the first printing sold out, making it a bestseller.

Darwin was pleased. However, now a different problem emerged.

While open-minded intellectuals praised the book, conservative religious leaders and upper-class nobility at once denounced Darwin's theory of natural selection.

Blasphemy! This book shows disrespect toward God!

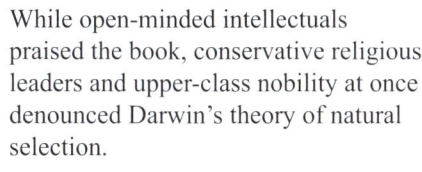

While the criticism grew, Darwin wrote letter upon letter, dozens every week, to those whom he thought would listen to him. Through his letters, Darwin sought to explain his theory of natural selection and convince others of its value.

08 Darwin, The Great Scientist

Track 28 ▶

Opposition to Darwin's book gradually grew stronger. He grew exhausted trying to persuade those who objected to his theory. Around the time the heated debate over evolution reached its peak, Darwin and his family took a vacation.

His daughter Henrietta had been ill, so they went to visit a relative so she could recuperate.

That leaf is eating an insect!

It's called a pitcher plant. They're carnivorous.

You mean there are carnivorous plants?

Darwin was captivated by this plant. He dug up a few and brought them back home. There he started a new experiment.

Look, it eats meat too.

There really are meat-eating plants. Amazing!

Darwin studied carnivorous plants for many years.

He then became fascinated with orchids.

Fatigued from controversy and trying to explain himself, Darwin now lived a live of seclusion, where he could concentrate on his experiments.

Meanwhile, Huxley had become a strong advocate of Darwin's theory of evolution, coming to the forefront in debates.

Humans evolved from their ape ancestors. Isn't the evidence clear enough?

Pack it in! We are all God's creations!

Darwin's the most dangerous person in England!

Darwin's supporters remained undaunted, continuing to spread the theory of evolution.

Huxley even coined a new word to describe Darwin's theory of evolution, "Darwinism".

This thory has the power to change the world. It's only right that it be called "Darwinism"

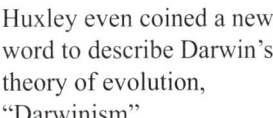

In 1862. Darwin published *the paper On the Various Contrivances By Which British and Foreign Orchids Are Fertilised By Insects.*

It's about how flowers have evolved in particular to attract insects.

I see. Well, I am currently writing Man's Place in Nature.

Oh! And I am writing The History of Man.

Actually, the content supports species variation.

Mine too.

Don't be a copycat.

My thoughts exactly.

In September 1863, while absorbed in Lyell's new book, *The Antiquity of Man*, Darwin suddenly became very ill.

Take him out to a nice place to rest, and give him cold baths daily. That should help his dermatitis.

Kaff!

171

However, the treatment the doctor advised was not beneficial, and Darwin's health further deteriorated.

There's really nothing more I can do at this point.

The ailing Darwin spent four years confined to his home, seeing hardly anybody.

Little did Darwin know that while he was struggling to survive he had become the most famous scientist in the world.

The Origin of Species was translated into various languages, allowing Darwin's theory to be known around the world.

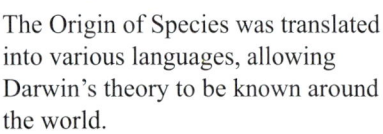

Scholars from various fields, including linguistics, economics, philosophy, and psychology applied the theory of evolution to their own research fields, further developing the theory.

Survival of the fittest. That's quite a good idea. Ha ha!

Spencer's theory was very popular, and before long people began using the phrase "survival of the fittest" when describing Darwin's theory of evolution.

They say the term "natural selection" is too difficult to understand.

Really?

When I next revise The Origin of Species, I guess I should include the term "survival of the fittest" too.

Well, in that case I'll need to collect the royalties in full.

Ha ha ha!

Darwin was still very ill, but he could not stop writing his book and continuing his research.

Darwin's reputation continued to grow, and he was recognized as one of the greatest scientists in the world.

By the latter half of 1860, the word "evolution" was no longer considered a taboo word in England.

Books on evolution are popping up everywhere. But none of them are satisfactory.

The atmosphere has matured, and it seems like now is the time to discuss the origins of man.

Darwin spent the next two years analyzing his observations, collecting the opinions of experts, and writing daily.

Then, in 1871 he published
The Descent of Man,
and Selection in Relation to Sex.

Humans were no different
from other species; they
also originated in
the microorganisms that
were around after
extinction.

I've wanted
to tell this story
for quite some
time now, but it's
come to this.

Darwin preferred to stay home and live
a quiet life with his family rather than
appear out in front of crowds of people.

In November 1877, Darwin received
an honorary doctorate from his
alma mater, Cambridge University.
Normally unconcerned about awards,
Darwin especially valued this prize.

Like Darwin, the other researcher of natural selection, Wallace, was also enjoying increased fame, as he spent his days teaching.

Professor Darwin, You gave humankind the gift of a new history.

Wallace, your efforts were also substantial.

Meanwhile, although Darwin was still ill, he never stopped working on his research and writing.

Today is the anniversary of the day your father passed away.

It's already that time of year again? I didn't even noticed the time passing.

Darwin's father, Robert Darwin, who always worried about his son growing up to be an honest, hardworking man, had passed away in 1848.

At the time, Darwin had been very sick, which caused him to arrive late to his hometown and miss his father's funeral.

Father, sniff, sniff…

After Darwin and Emma married, they had ten children, including Henrietta, George, Elizabeth, and Francis.

Emma devotedly took care of Darwin throughout his periods of illness. She supported his ideas, and faithfully fulfilled her role as mother and wife.

Darwin continued his research until the day he died. In his final years of life he turned his focus toward earthworms.

These are necessary for soil to support plant growth.

Earthworms can be found in the ground all over the world.

So much so that most of the dirt forming the Earth's surface is actually made of earthworm waste.

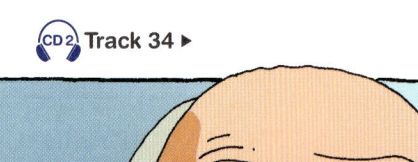

Earthworms vigorously eat dead plants, and then leave their waste behind.

For hundreds of years the multitude of earthworms on the Earth's surface fed on dead plants, leaving their excrement behind. This accumulated waste became fertile soil, which allowed plants to grow and thrive.

Darwin wrote about these findings in another book, *The Formation of Vegetable Mould Through the Action of Worms*.

Of all your books, Professor, the one about earthworms sells the best.

You mean not The Origin of Species?

After completing his earthworm research and related writing, Darwin suffered a heart attack.

Honey!

I believe it's time for my flame to burn out.

No, Dear. Don't speak like that!

Don't weep, Emma. I'm not afraid.

I will always love you, Charles!

I love you too.

In April of 1882 Darwin had a more severe heart attack and passed away. He was 73 years old.

Darwin is buried next to Sir Isaac Newton in Westminster Abbey, London, England. Darwin's theory changed the world, and he set the groundwork from which modern biology developed. Moreover, Darwin will forever be remembered as a great scientist who turned the study of evolution into a scientific discipline and then worked to prove the theory scientifically.

The Origin of Species

As you know,
my book *The Origin of Species* consists of
15 chapters. Here I briefly explain each one.

Chapter 1 introduces Variation Under
Domestication. When living things are
placed in a novel environment,
variations occur over generations.

For example, compared to wild ducks,
ducks raised domestically have lighter wing bones and
heavier leg bones because domesticated ducks have flown
less and walked much more than wild ducks.

Thus. through changes in behavior,
animals use some body parts more than others,
causing the structure of their bodies to change.
These changed body parts are then
passed on to their offspring.

*Darwin's assertion here is known as
"the theory of use and disuse," or "Lamarckism."
It was later proven to be false.

It is clear that offspring inherit their physical characteristics from their parents.
However, the process by which heredity occurs is still unclear.
Nobody knows why, for example,
the same traits are inherited in some cases, but not in others.
why a trait is present in one generation and not in the next,
but then reappears in the following generation?
why is a trait present in only one parent inherited by
only one of the sexes among is offspring?

I decided to investigate these questions by observing pigeons.
I raised every variety of pigeon I could find.

My investigation of many pigeon varieties revealed that
their facial bone structure differed greatly. I also found many differences
in the number of bones in the back, ribs and tail feathers:
the length of their wings. tails, legs and feet: the size of their eggs,
their method of flight and their calls. These various types of pigeons,
which developed for a variety of needs, had each changed in
a unique way. In fact, scienatists would see them and
claim they were different bird species.

Animals and plants raised domestically change
not according to what is best for them,
but to the particular tastes of man.
Man has used these endlessly occurring
mutations to his advantage.

However, in generally, mutations that are advantageous to man do not occur often.
Thus. to increase the probabilty of advantageous mutations,
the number of organisms must be high.
Tree cultivators and livestock breeders produce large
numbers of trees and livestock to create
new *varieties to increase profits.

*Variety: A new variation of a species in which only specific traits have
changed due to the accumulation of changes in the environment.

186

Chapter 2 of *The Origin of Species*
explains variation under nature.
Even in nature, a great variety of mutations occur.

Two people who seem the same are actually
not exactly the same. Hair color and style,
skin color, and height can all be different.
I call these minor differences
"individual differences".
I believe these individual differences are
very important because they are the first steps
toward the divergence of varieties.

New species often begin as *geographical race,
which eventually become completely new species.
However, not all new varieties become new pecies.
Some are pushed to extinction by other varieties, while others
remain as varieties without becoming new species.

*Geographical race: A group of a particular species separated geographically
  from other groups.

Chapter 3 describes the struggle for existence.
Mutations beneficial to organisms will assist them
in survival and be passed on to their offspring.
In this way, mutations beneficial to survival are preserved.
I have named this process "natural selection" to
differentiate it from selection caused by humans.

There are many varieties of the struggle for life.
For example, when food is scarce, two animals belonging to
the same family will compete for the available food.
The struggle for existence occurs because organisms produce
large numbers of offspring that greatly outnumber the number
that can actually survive and thus,
organisms must fight with others of the same species,
other species and even the environment.
This reflects the application of *Malthus' principle
of population to all plants and animals.

*Malthus' Principle of Population: While populations increase by geometric
 progression, food supplies increase only at a constant rate. For this reason,
if a population is not controlled, its weaker members will not be able to
acquire food and will die off.

There are many factors preventing the number of
individuals in a population from increasing, such as a limited
food and being preyed upon by other animals.
Climate is also an important factor, and contagious diseases
can also limit population increase.

Chapter 4 describes natural selection in detail.
Just as man controls the mutations of other organisms to
their advantage, organisms themselves have the potential
to mutate in ways beneficial to them.

Regardless of how small the mutation is,
it will allow the organism to obtain a more beneficial position
for survival and reproduction to the extent it is beneficial to an organism.
Humans cause organisms to change to meet
human needs, but nature causes change
for the benefit of the organisms themselves.
Furthermore. humans are more interested
in external changes in organisms,
while natural selection applies to all parts
of organisms, both internal and external.

When causing mutations. nature eliminates
bad traits and preserves good traits to better
match organisms with the conditions for life.
For example, insects that eat tree leaves are green,
while insects that eat the trunks and
branches are gray to help them blend in.
Thus nature causes organisms to both evolve
and devolve for the sake of survival.

Chapter 5 deals with the laws of mutation.
It is commonly thought that mutations occur by chance,
but actually the mechanism behind mutations is
simply still unknown; it does not happens
completely by chance.

Shellfish that live in southern seas or shallow waters are
lighter in color than those of northern seas or deep waters.
Moreover, the leaves of plants growing on the coast
have thicker leaves than plants living in other areas.
Why do these changes occur?

Let's look at some other examples.
The often-used body parts of domestic animals
become larger and stronger, while those parts
become smaller and weaker.
These changes are passed on to future
generations. For example, the wings of birds
with no natural meat-eating enemies will
gradually become smaller and devolve.

Organisms can live not only in the area on their birth,
but can also adapt to live in other climates.
This phenomenon is not due to chance,
but rather because organisms are
born with the ability to adapt to
other climates.

Organisms with a lower level of evolution
mutate more easily than those with a higher level.
If a body part of a particular species is
exceptionally different from the same part
of another member of the same class.
then the probability is high
that the body part has mutated.

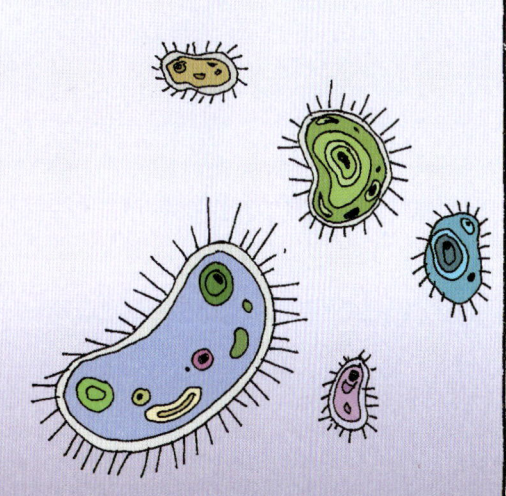

There are also analogous mutations,
that is, two different species will sometimes exhibit similar mutations.
This shows how two different varieties of organisms may have
the same ancestors, from which they inherited the same traits.

Chapter 6 of *The Origin of Species* explains some of
the questions surrounding the theory of natural selection.
For example, if a particular species changes into a different species through
various stages of change, why do we not see all the different transitional
forms of the species?
Furthermore, is it possible for a ground-dwelling animal
to change into an animal with a completely different structure
and behavior, such as a bat?

The reason it is difficult to find examples of
the transitional forms of species is because
advantageous mutations have a strong
tendency to exclude less advantageous
mutations from being inherited.
By the time a new species emerges its ancestors
and earlier variations have been weeded out,
with all similar varieties having died out.

There is also the issue of whether it is possible for
land animals to live in the water.
A closer look at organisms, however,
reveals that in addition to organisms that can only
live on land and those that can only live in water,
there are also organisms that can live in
both environments.

River otters have webbed feet, but their fur coat,
short legs and tail are all similar to those of sea otters.
In the summer. they live in water and feed on fish,
while in the winter they will live on land and eat
small animals such as rodents.

Let's now look at how a four-legged animal could change into a flying bat.
Animals belonging to the squirrel family, for example,
are found in a variety of traits, including flat tails,
wide lower bodies, and bulging flanks. In particular,
flying squirrels can spread their skin wide to fly from tree to tree.
These traits, which were beneficial to squirrels in escaping from
animals of prey, accumulated over numerous generations of mutations,
eventually resulting in what we new.

Chapter 7 discusses the objections raised in
response to the theory of natural selection.
The geologist Mivart originally supported my theory,
but he later became a fierce critic.
Even though he could understand, for example,
the survival of organisms with fully developed eyes and wings,
Mivart wondered how organisms
with less than fully developed eyes and wings
were able to survive.

Other scholars, such as Kelvin, Owen and Jenkin,
also voiced their opposing views regarding my theory.
Kelvin believed that the Earth's history was much
too short for the slow process of evolution to occur.
He believed the Earth was only tens
of millions of years old.

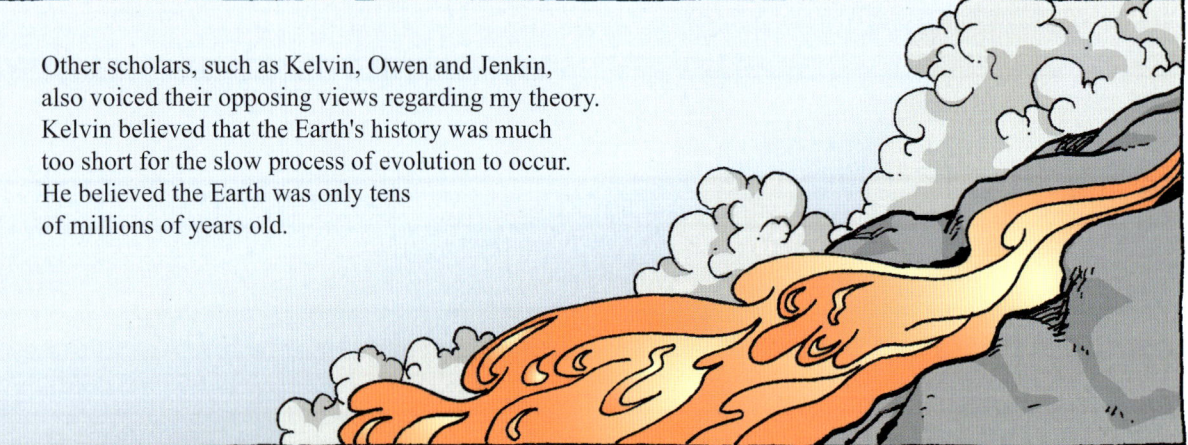

Jenkin proposed that even if an individual organism
has a trait beneficial to survival,
if that organism mates with an organism without that trait,
then the trait will not be passed on to the offspring.
However, this suggestion was proven false by
experiments conducted by the geneticist Mendel.

Chapter 8 explains instinct. Instincts are actions beneficial to survival performed by all members of a species in the same way without their knowing for what purpose they are performed.
I believe that instincts are passed on to an organism's offspring in the same way physical characteristics are transmitted.

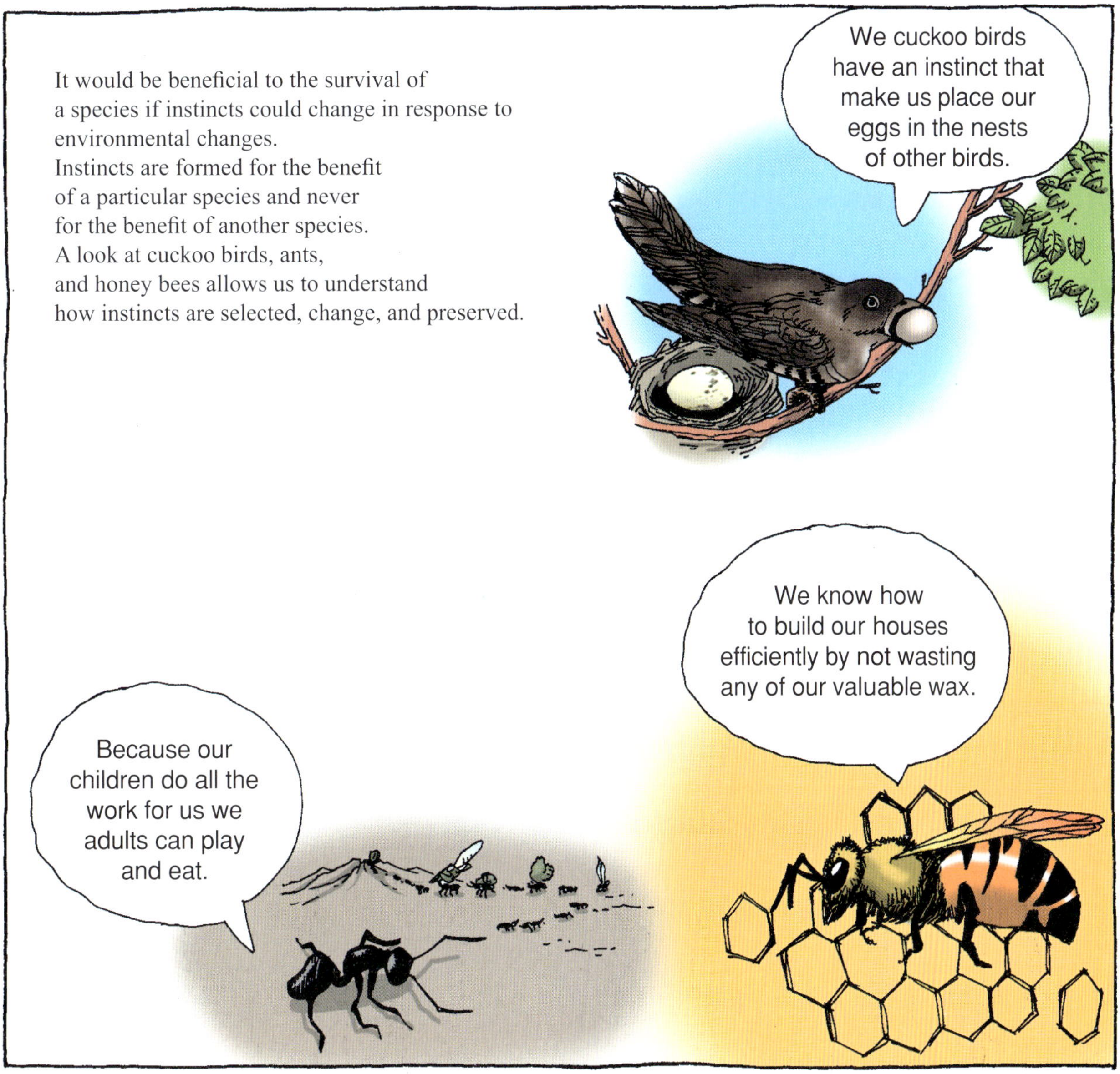

It would be beneficial to the survival of a species if instincts could change in response to environmental changes.
Instincts are formed for the benefit of a particular species and never for the benefit of another species.
A look at cuckoo birds, ants, and honey bees allows us to understand how instincts are selected, change, and preserved.

We cuckoo birds have an instinct that make us place our eggs in the nests of other birds.

We know how to build our houses efficiently by not wasting any of our valuable wax.

Because our children do all the work for us we adults can play and eat.

Chapter 9 explains hybridism.
If two species are very close genetically
they can crossbreed and some of their offspring
will be able to have children.

Chapter 10 discusses the imperfection
of the geological record.
There are various cases of the absence of intermediate
varieties in geological formations.
It is clear that intermediate varieties existed in the past
even if they cannot be found.
However, because very old ancestors and their present-day
descendants are very different,
it is extremely difficult to find related matches.
Moreover, the geological record is too imperfect to be
reliable.

The Earth has a very long history and
for this reason sedimentary layers have become
very thick over the passage of time.
The reason it is hard to locate intermediate fossils is
because the remaining geological record is incomplete.

Chapter 11 is about the geologic succession of organic beings. Even if the geological record is incomplete, the existence of fossils nonetheless provides support for the theory that all species have a common ancestor. For example, fossils linking the ancestors of completely different species, such as horses and pigs, have been discovered.

Chapters 12 and 13 explain geographical distribution, a topic heavily debated among scholars.
The main point of contention is whether species were created in only one particular area of the Earth or in multiple areas.

There is a convincing argument to be made for all species emerging from one geographical area and then spreading to other, distant areas. It is difficult, but not possible, to determine how species moved from one location to another.

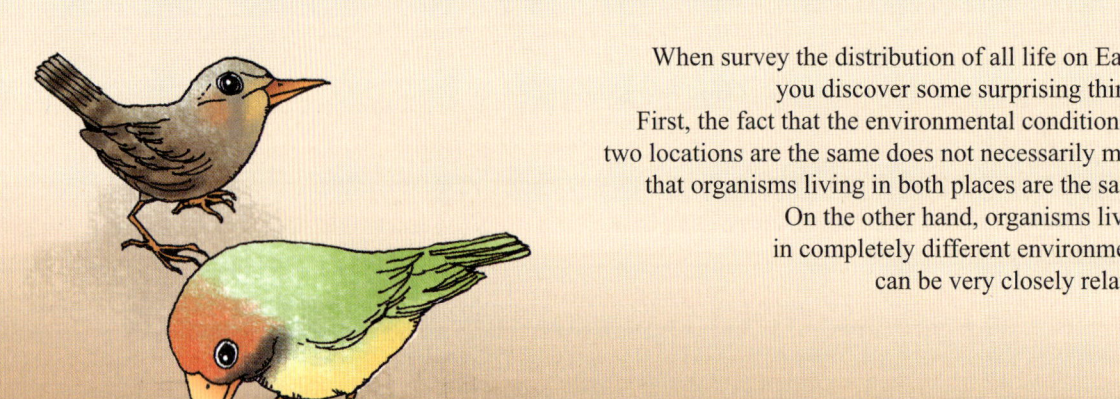

When survey the distribution of all life on Earth,
you discover some surprising things.
First, the fact that the environmental conditions of
two locations are the same does not necessarily mean
that organisms living in both places are the same.
On the other hand, organisms living
in completely different environments
can be very closely related.

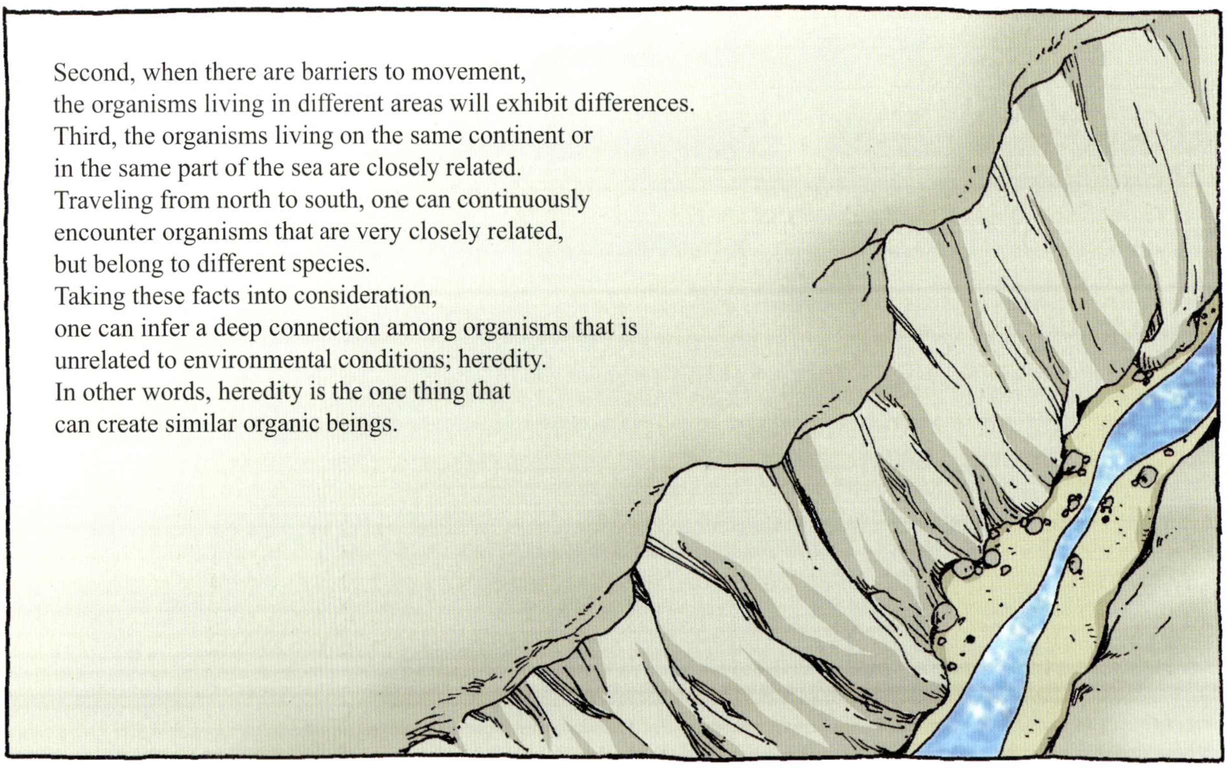

Second, when there are barriers to movement,
the organisms living in different areas will exhibit differences.
Third, the organisms living on the same continent or
in the same part of the sea are closely related.
Traveling from north to south, one can continuously
encounter organisms that are very closely related,
but belong to different species.
Taking these facts into consideration,
one can infer a deep connection among organisms that is
unrelated to environmental conditions; heredity.
In other words, heredity is the one thing that
can create similar organic beings.

Climate change had a big influence on the movement of organisms.
Even areas currently inhospitable to life may have been easily
occupied by life in the past, under a different climate.
The elevation of land also likely had an influence on the movement
of life. Furthermore, in the past, islands may have been connected to
other islands, while continents may have also been linked together
such that organisms could easily cross them.

Although the number of species living on remote islands in large oceans is smaller than the number living on a continent within the same amount of land area, the proportion of unique species on the islands is greater. Animals that migrated into such isolated areas likely mutated more easily through competition with the native species already living there, subsequently passing their mutations on to their offspring.

Chapter 14 explains the similarities of organic beings, including morphology, embryology, and rudimentary organs. From long ago in the past until the present day, organisms diverged along various branches. These organisms can be grouped according to similar characteristics, and then categorized into groups subordinate to other groups. Through such classification based on morphology, embryology and rudimentary organs, all life on earth can be classified by group and eventually traced back to the same ancestor.

Chapter 15 summarizes and concludes the book. I have no doubts about what I have written in *The Origin of Species*. However, I cannot expect my peers, who have spent years researching theories in opposition to mine, to suddenly accept my theory. Nonetheless, whoever believe species are mutable should conscientiously expressing that conviction, for that will mean that the prejudices toward the theory of natural selection will have begun to disappear little by little.

Word Search

● Find the words which are hidden horizontally, vertically and diagonally.

```
C M Z G Q M Z G Q M Z G Q Q M Z G Q M X
W E C I E N T I S T N H W W N A H C N V
E N M J P E R S E V E R A N C E I O B A
R V F P R D C K R V K R R B C K M V L
E I U O A S D O M E S T I C A T E I C E
V R L Q Y N Z O Y X N Q Y Y O E N O X D
E O F W U C I W C Z G W R U A P J N Z I
A N I E I A O O I A E P E I D U A E A C
L M L R C S G N N S L H H O S R S R S T
T E L U P O H T T D I Y O P D S T B D O
A N R Y H F E Y A R C S V A F U Y I F R
S T S U S T I D N R I I E I N I U T V I
T H S I D H M O D O L V R D H T I Y O A
O J A B S O I A F F T I A F J T J F Y N
R K N P R T P O R F I A N N T E B G A I
H L A W A W A R D S Y N H H C E N H G B
J Q T I J Q T A U P C O R I T E M J E L
L W R Q L W Y Q L R Y Q L L W Y Q L U E
Z A R E V E N T Z I K F Z Z S U F T J R
V E M E X M R I N N P O E T U R E X N M
W R E M O V E C P G O P H T R Q C I R P
```

| perseverance | environment | contrivance | domesticate |
| variation | offspring | pursuit | voyage |

Vocabulary

Lesson 2

● Match each word to the correct meaning.

1. dedication   • 관찰

2. extinction   • 종

3. embark   • 멸종

4. observation   • 헌신

5. revolution   • 진화

6. theology   • 인지

7. species   • 물려받다

8. evolution   • 논쟁하다

9. fervent   • 혁명

10. dispute   • 출항하다

11. recognition   • 신학

12. inherit   • 열렬한

Guess What?

• Guess what she said in the blank.

Charles' father, Robert Darwin, was a very sympathetic man with a keen intuition.

I wonder why Charles likes to wander outside so much?

A respectable physician, he began treating patients around the age of 21 and was very successful at it.

He has no interest in studying and cares about nothing other than hunting around for rodents. This is serious.

Oh, Father!

Why did you take just one bird egg?

Endangered Animals

Endangered animals are those species that are in danger of extinction. Today so many species are vanishing from the Earth each year, at a rate faster than the mass extinctions of dinosaurs about 6 million years ago. Galapagos penguins and Galapagos giant tortoises which Darwin observed in 1835 are also one of the endangered species now. These are some of the endangered animals on the Earth.

Polar bear
북극곰

Galapagos tortoise
갈라파고스 거북

Galapagos penguin
갈라파고스 펭귄

Orangutan
오랑우탄

© Thomas Lersch

Chimpanzee
침팬지

© Mila Zinkora

Western gorilla
서부 고릴라

Voyage on the Beagle

상트 페테르부르크의 동물학 박물관에 있는 비글호 모형

From December 27, 1831 to October 2, 1836, Charles Robert Darwin served as naturalist and unpaid assistant on the ship Beagle. During the five-year voyage around the world, Darwin observed and studied nature through a tremendous variety of plants and animals. These observations and studies led him to his theory of natural selection. This voyage changed not only Darwin's life and thought but also the general thinking about natural history and even the course of science.

비글호에 승선했던 풍경화가 콘래드 마르텐스가 그린 그림

유네스코 세계자연유산 갈라 파고스 제도

산티아고
산타크루즈
페르난디나
이사벨라
산크리스토발

갈라파고스 지도

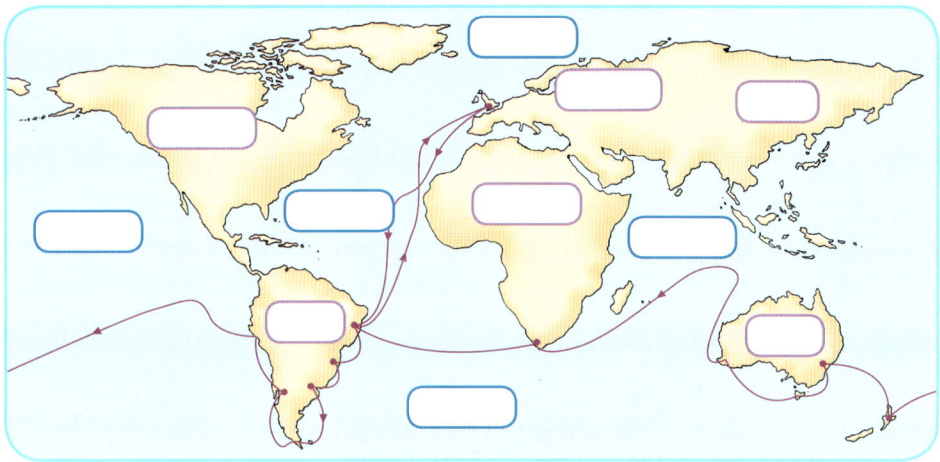

비글호의 이동 경로

1. Label each continent on the map.

> North America   Africa   Asia
>
> South America   Europe   Australia

2. Label each ocean on the map.

> The Pacific Ocean   The Atlantic Ocean
>
> The Indian Ocean   The Artic Ocean   The Antartic Ocean

3. Thinking about the importance of Darwin's voyage, follow the route of the *Beagle* on the map, starting from England in 1831 until he arrived back in England in 1836.

연표

1809년   2월 12일, 영국 슈롭셔 주의 슈루즈버리에서 태어났습니다.

1818년 9세   슈루즈버리에 있는 버틀러 박사의 기숙 학교에 입학합니다.

1825년 16세   스코틀랜드에 있는 에든버러 대학에서 의학 공부를 시작하지만 의학 보다 박물학과 지질학에 흥미를 느낍니다.

1828년 19세   케임브리지 신학 대학에 입학합니다.

1831년 22세   해군 측량선 비글호에 박물학자로 승선해 달라는 제의를 받고, 그 해 12월, 비글호를 타고 남아메리카로 향합니다.

1834년 25세   파타고니아, 마젤란 해협 부근, 안데스 산맥 산록부를 탐사합니다.

1835년 26세   갈라파고스 제도에 약 4주 간 머무르며 핀치 새 표본을 채집합니다.

1836년 27세   5년 간의 항해를 끝내고 10월 2일 영국에 도착하여 10월 4일 슈루즈 버리의 고향집에 도착합니다.

1838년 29세   토머스 맬서스의 『인구론』에서 결정적인 단서를 얻어 종에 관한 연구 를 계속합니다.

1839년 30세   왕립협회 회원이 됩니다.

1839년 30세   엠마 웨지우드와 결혼합니다.

1840년 31세   건강이 좋지 않아 가족과 함께 런던 교외 다운으로 이사합니다.

1846년	**37세**	비글호 항해에서 돌아온 지 10년 만에 모든 표본들의 정리를 끝냅니다.
1848년	**39세**	다윈의 아버지가 세상을 떠납니다.
1856년	**47세**	종에 관한 방대한 저서를 집필하기 시작합니다.
1858년	**49세**	앨프리드 월리스가 보낸 연구 보고서를 받고 자신의 생각과 비슷한 것을 알게 됩니다. 『종의 기원』 저술을 보류하고 런던의 린네 학회에서 논문 『종의 변종 형성의 경향과 자연 선택에 의한 종과 변종의 영속성에 관하여』를 월리스와 함께 발표하지만 관심을 얻지 못합니다.
1859년	**50세**	11월 22일, 『자연선택에 의한 종의 기원에 관하여』를 출간합니다. 초판 1250부가 당일로 매진되며 엄청난 파문을 일으킵니다.
1862년	**53세**	『곤충에 의해 수정되는 영국과 외국 난의 여러 가지 고안에 관하여』를 출간합니다.
1863년	**54세**	건강이 악화됩니다.
1864년	**55세**	왕립협회로부터 코프레이 메달을 받습니다.
1871년	**62세**	『인간의 유래와 성과 관련한 선택』을 출간합니다.
1872년	**63세**	『인간과 동물의 감정 표현』을 출간합니다. 『종의 기원』 제6판에서 처음으로 '진화'라는 용어를 사용합니다.
1882년	**73세**	4월 19일, 73세의 나이로 세상을 떠나 4월 26일, 웨스트민스터 대성당 묘지에 묻힙니다.

Biography Comic **who?**

who? 01	Barack Obama	978-89-6370-514-9
who? 02	Charles Darwin	978-89-6370-515-6
who? 03	Bill Gates	978-89-6370-516-3
who? 04	Hillary Clinton	978-89-6370-517-0
who? 05	Stephen Hawking	978-89-6370-518-7
who? 06	Oprah Winfrey	978-89-6370-519-4
who? 07	Steven Spielberg	978-89-6370-520-0
who? 08	Thomas Edison	978-89-6370-521-7
who? 09	Abraham Lincoln	978-89-6370-522-4
who? 10	Martin Luther King, Jr.	978-89-6370-523-1
who? 11	Louis Braille	978-89-6370-439-5
who? 12	Albert Einstein	978-89-6370-440-1
who? 13	Jane Goodall	978-89-6370-441-8
who? 14	Walt Disney	978-89-6370-442-5
who? 15	Winston Churchill	978-89-6370-443-2
who? 16	Warren Buffett	978-89-6370-444-9
who? 17	Nelson Mandela	978-89-6370-445-6
who? 18	Steve Jobs	978-89-6370-446-3
who? 19	J. K. Rowling	978-89-6370-447-0
who? 20	Jean-Henri Fabre	978-89-6370-448-7
who? 21	Vincent van Gogh	978-89-6370-449-4
who? 22	Marie Curie	978-89-6370-450-0
who? 23	Henry David Thoreau	978-89-6370-451-7
who? 24	Andrew Carnegie	978-89-6370-452-4
who? 25	Coco Chanel	978-89-6370-453-1
who? 26	Charlie Chaplin	978-89-6370-454-8
who? 27	Ho Chi Minh	978-89-6370-455-5
who? 28	Ludwig van Beethoven	978-89-6370-456-2
who? 29	Mao Zedong	978-89-6370-457-9
who? 30	Kim Dae-jung	978-89-6370-458-6